PURRFECT PARENTING

By Beverly Guhl
with Don H. Fontenelle, Ph.D.
Illustrations by Beverly Guhl

FISHER BOOKS

Library of Congress Cataloging-in-Publication Data
Guhl, Beverly
     Purrfect Parenting

     "A seriously humorous and humorously serious book for parents"
     —Cover
     Includes index.
     1. Parenting—United States—Anecdotes, facetiae, satire, etc.
2. Parent and child—United States—Anecdotes, facetiae, satire, etc.
I. Fontenelle, Don, 1946 –   . II. Title.
HQ755.8.G84   1987   649'.64'0207   87-8819
ISBN 1-55561-004-8 (pbk.)

Publishers: Howard W. Fisher & Fred W. Fisher
Coordinator: Veronica Durie
Editor: Judith Schuler
Art Director: Josh Young

Published by Fisher Books
3499 N. Campbell Avenue, Suite 909
Tucson, Arizona 85719
(602) 325-5263

Notice: The information in this book is true and complete to the best of our knowledge. It is offered with no guarantees on the part of the authors or Fisher Books. The authors and publisher disclaim all liability in connection with use of this book.

Table of Contents...

For Gary, Jon and Asa
Beverly Guhl

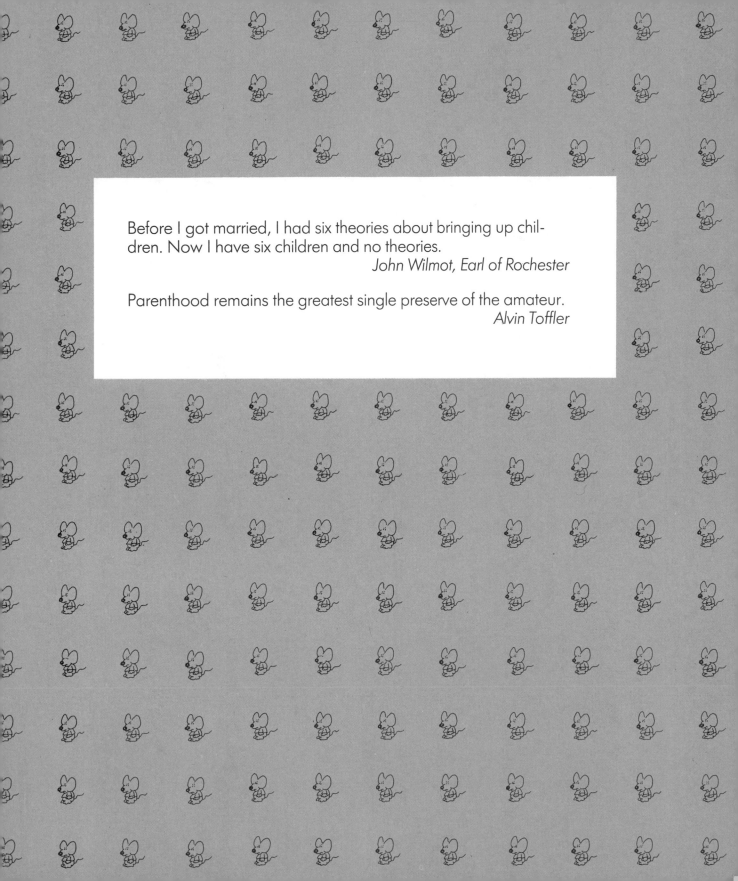

Before I got married, I had six theories about bringing up children. Now I have six children and no theories.

John Wilmot, Earl of Rochester

Parenthood remains the greatest single preserve of the amateur.

Alvin Toffler

Is Your Home Infested with Brats?

Yes, folks, it's that time of year again. Brat-warning season. Parents all over are finding their homes infested with these ornery critters. Brats come in all shapes and sizes! But what do **brats** look like, and how do you tell if **your** home is infested? Go over this helpful checklist, and you'll find out!

Brat-Infestation Checklist *Warning signs include:*

• Toys, clothing, personal items littering house that don't belong to you.
• Loud noises, crying, screaming, fighting, whining, name-calling, rock music, MTV on too much.
• Items vanishing mysteriously without permission, such as foodstuffs or scissors. (Anything missing?)
• Uncontrollable situations or behavior disturbances, such as tantrums and flying objects.
• Mysterious messes appearing within minutes of cleaning up.
• TV, lights and appliances left on or telephone tied up for hours.

Any of the above signs is an indication you have a serious, or potentially serious, brat infestation in your home! If left untreated, it could get worse!

Simple, effective brat-eradication treatments are available today (and outlined herein). Please follow instructions carefully. Adjust dosages accordingly. Wear "kid gloves" when handling brat specimens you may find.

Please note: Brat activity may intensify at first. This is normal. Continue treatments to ensure results!

Timetables for complete brat eradication vary, depending on the degree of infestation and how long left untreated. Continue treatments as often as necessary to avoid reinfestation.

UNIVERSAL TRUTHS OF PARENTING...

TRUTH NUMBER ONE

ONE CHILD IS NOT ENOUGH,
BUT TWO IS WAY TOO MANY.

TRUTH NUMBER TWO

BABIES ARE ADORABLE,
BUT THEY DO GROW UP.

TRUTH NUMBER THREE

YOU CAN'T LIVE WITH CHILDREN,
AND YOU CAN'T LIVE WITHOUT THEM.

THE PARENT

Par-ent (per' nt) n. 1. a father or mother 2. any organism in relation to its offspring. (If you're like most parents, definition 2 best describes you—not by choice but because your kids usually **treat** you like an **organism!**)

Anatomy of the Organism

1. **Brain**—Center of pseudointellectual thought. Prone to headaches.
2. **Eyebrows**—Used to express emotions, execute non-verbal commands. Said to be the mirror of the brain.
3. **Eyes**—Inconsistent. Never see what they should, and see things they shouldn't.
4. **Ears**—Hypersensitive to whining and hard-rock music.
5. **Nose**—Flares accordingly when organism is angered. Able to "smell trouble."
6. **Vocal cords**—Complete octave range. Frequently tested to maximum.
7. **Skin**—Impervious to penetration by young teeth.
8. **Heart**—Too soft or too hard. Frequently "broken."
9. **Arms**—Very strong. Used for dragging brats to bed or out of stores.
10. **Hands**—Contradictory. Instruments of care or corporal punishment.
11. **Stomach**—Strong. Capable of withstanding sight of runny-nosed child.
12. **Legs**—Very fast. Used to chase down small wrongdoers.
13. **Shins**—Tough. Capable of withstanding repeated kicks delivered by persons under 3' tall.
14. **Feet**—Impervious to pain when stomped on by angry little persons.

A BRIEF INTRODUCTION

The role of being a parent carries with it complex duties. Most of us receive no training for this difficult task!

Yet we quickly think of ourselves as authorities on our children! After all, we were once children ourselves! But we don't become an authority on computers by once having been a computer. Rather we **learn** how! With this book you can learn to reprogram your systems and take the byte out of the brat, thereby making yourself (and your children) user-friendly!

Each child is **unique!** It comes with a mind of its own, a personality of its own, a temper of its own, requires no batteries, operates 24 hours a day, 7 days a week and . . . worst of all . . . no money-back guarantee!

Children have different personalities. We can't deal with all of them using the same methods or assume the type of discipline that works with one child will work with his brother or sister!

HOUSEBREAKING

Can You Teach a New Dog New Tricks?
Yes, and you can teach an older dog new tricks, too. We're going to equip you with ways to change your dog's, er, child's, behavior, whether the child is very young or about to leave the doghouse on its own.

Who's Teaching Whom?
A brat doesn't become a brat overnight nor does he become one mysteriously with no assistance from us! Teaching is a two-way street.

The plus side is if we can teach our children to be brats, we can also teach them to be good!

RUFFY'S REWARD

A Comedy of Errors?

In the true-life drama presented above, what really happened? Ruffy wanted a biscuit. Mommy said no. Ruffy had a tantrum. Mommy got angry. The tantrum escalated. Mommy finally behaved and gave Ruffy his biscuit!

My, doesn't Ruffy have a well-trained mommy? Ruffy knows exactly what will make her do what he wants. But wait a minute! Hasn't mommy trained Ruffy to misbehave? She's shown Ruffy if he really wants something bad enough, all he has to do is throw a tantrum, and it's **biscuit city!**

ANATOMY OF A TANTRUM

As Easy as A-B-C!

For every situation, there is a cause, an: **Antecedent**

Causes are followed by: **Behavior**

Behavior is followed by: **Consequence**

A

Ruffy is told "No!"

B

Ruffy has a tantrum.

C

Ruffy gets a biscuit.

Q: Why does Ruffy behave this way?
A: Because it gets him what he wants.

The consequence—getting the biscuit—is actually a **reward** for the tantrum!

The good news—You have just learned to **analyze behavior!**

The bad news—You have just learned **you** are **part** of the behavior!

Children are unpredictable. You never know what inconsistency they're going to catch you in next.

Franklin P. Jones

The persons hardest to convince they're at the retirement age are children at bedtime.

Shannon Fife

BLUEPRINT FOR A BRAT

THE FOLLOWING ARE DIFFERENT PLANS YOU CAN EMPLOY TO ACHIEVE THE BRAT OF YOUR DREAMS! EACH PLAN HAS BEEN THOROUGHLY PARENT-CHILD TESTED FOR GENERATIONS, AND SATISFACTION IS GUARANTEED.

PLAN A — Meaningless Threats (a.k.a. B.S.)

Make statements you don't mean or threats you'll never carry out! This is foolproof and won't stop the behavior!

IF YOU KIDS DON'T STOP FIGHTING, I'M GOING TO TIE YOUR TAILS TOGETHER AND THROW YOU OUT THE WINDOW!!

STOP THAT SQUEALING RIGHT THIS MINUTE OR I'LL BE MAKIN' BACON OUT OF YOU!!!!

PLAN D | Ping-Ponging

Put the kid in an endless loop of "Go ask your mother—go ask your father."
Or let the kid play one parent against the other! This produces con artists—
something the world has a tragic shortage of.

PLAN F — Random Discipline (a.k.a. Bushwhacking or Ambushing)

Don't warn the kid in advance what the punishment will be! Wait till the rule is broken or he misbehaves, **then** act irrationally and out of anger. Punish the daylights out of him! This is so viciously unfair, it's sure to make the kid hate you and not feel responsible for his own actions. He won't feel in control of the consequences of his behavior—you'll get all the blame!

AH-HA!! YOU'RE HOME ONE HOUR LATE!... JUST FOR **THAT**, YOU ARE GROUNDED FOR A MONTH!!

THAT'S UNBEARABLE!! IF I'D KNOWN YOU WERE GOING TO DO THAT I'D HAVE BEEN HOME ONE HOUR EARLY!!!!

AS TEMPTING AS ALL THE ABOVE PLANS ARE, LET'S FACE IT THERE ARE ALREADY ENOUGH BRATS IN THE WORLD, SO WHO NEEDS YOUR CONTRIBUTION??!!!!

Consistency

THE C-TEAM

In "Blueprint for a Brat," we saw how inconsistent behavior creates brats! **We** don't listen to an adult who says one thing but does another, so why should our kids? Therefore, consistency is the foundation for brat eradication! Parents must be predictable as individuals, so **don't say anything you can't or don't want to do. Follow through with everything you say! Hang tough**—No leniency! Consistency is necessary from **both** parents as a **unit.** This is best achieved through teamwork!

THE C-TEAM SLOGAN: "Truth, Justice and the Consistency Way!"

* costumes optional!

Consistency and brat eradication comes from **both** parents being a **unit!** Each must:

- Mean what they say.
- Support each other.
- Agree on rules for the kids' behavior.
- Oppose brathood and dedicate their parenthood to stomping out inconsistencies.

THE C-TEAM IN ACTION!

Red Alert! Non-unity produces numerous booby traps! It undermines and reduces parental authority, teaches the kid to play one parent against the other and to manipulate to get his way. The kid then sees one parent as the "good guy" and the other as the "bad guy." This inconsistency promotes arguments between the team, which can make the kid feel responsible. **That** is too-heavy a trip to lay on a kid (no matter how rotten he may be)! If you disagree about something, support each other in public. After all, you can always arm wrestle about it later in private. So get your team in gear and remember—smart teams avoid booby traps!

Consequences

TEAM TACTICS

Save your breath, your energy and the brat's behind—just bring in the heavy artillery—ICBM's (inner-child behavior modifiers)*.
*Also known as: **consequences!**
The smart team has at its disposal a virtually unlimited supply of ammo for brat eradication! Consequences are **the big ones!** Found existing in nature, consequences can be used in their natural form or readily modified to become the most effective means of brat eradication on the face of the earth!

Above are the **three major consequences** you can use. Each has its own devastatingly effective usage in brat-control procedures!

BALANCE OF POWER

This balance of power is easily achieved. Rules or expectations for behavior can be set up in advance. They should be very specific. Spell it out in detail. Leave no loopholes!
Same for the consequences. Be specific! When a rule is broken, the kid already knows what to expect. All you need to do is follow through—and try not to smile.

WHO'S RESPONSIBLE . . .

It is **very important** for the little monster to realize he is responsible for his own behavior! If good things happen to him, it's because of him. If bad things happen, it's also because of him! He is responsible for the consequences of his behavior. If he knows he is responsible, then **he** can change the situation. He can make things better for himself, or worse! On the other hand, if he feels like his mean, horrible parents are in control, then they get the blame. He feels mistreated, and his condition is hopeless! Who needs it? So . . .

Don't wait till the last irrational minute to decide—**plan ahead!** State the consequence **before** the rule is broken, then sit back and let the kid choose his fate! (Why should you always be the heavy?)

A TACTICAL DIAGRAM

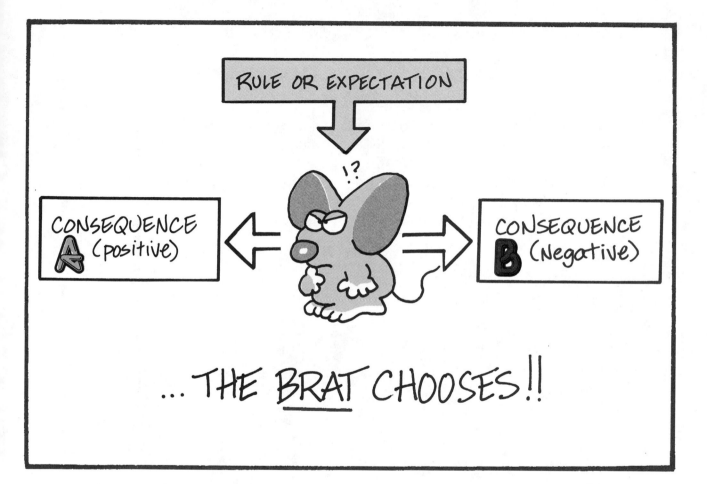

On the following pages, you'll see how this tactical diagram can be put into real-life action! You'll be ecstatic to note in each case the kid has a **choice**— he decides his fate! This eliminates nagging, threats, screaming, hostility, guilt, biting and bloodshed! **You're** in total control, but it is the kid who chooses the consequence for his behavior. **He** can make himself happy or sad with **his choice.** Such a deal!

Natural Consequences—
Harvesting natural resources!

Most often overlooked are consequences that surround us and the **brat!** Consequences so ingenious we wish we could have thought of them ourselves! Who wouldn't love to zap a monster headache onto a screaming brat? Well, take heart. Rest your overworked brain! After all, why should you waste valuable time devising hideously fair consequences when you can harvest these natural resources at every possible opportunity?

Grandma's Rule—
First do what I want, then you can do what you want!

Spontaneous and easy to use, this system has proven popular and reliable through the ages. How many of us were aware our grandmother was employing clever psychological tactics when she said, "Eat your meat and potatoes, then you can have some dessert!" Wow! You, too, can amaze your offspring with this sneaky technique. This works best when there is some type of activity involved that is of great interest to the brat!

Different Strokes—
One kid's trash is another's treasure!

These consequences are manmade or mommy/daddy-made. They're customized based on the individuality and personality of the brat in question! They can be positive or negative—anything that will produce the desired result. No two brats are created equal, not even sibling brats! So find those special things each individual brat hates most and loves most. Use them wisely and to your supreme advantage whenever necessary!

Because no two kids are alike, consequences must be individualized to work on each child's unique personality. Witness the following testimonials.*

Children have more need of models than of critics.

Joseph Joubert

Children have never been very good at listening to elders, but they have never failed to imitate them.

James Baldwin

Punishment

"It's a nasty job, but somebody's gotta do it!!" . . .

Punishment can best be described as **negative consequences,** something the child views as unenjoyable or the withdrawal of something positive. The emphasis here is on bad behavior. Punishments range from screaming at a kid to spanking him, and many things in between. There are **constructive** forms of punishment, and there are **destructive** forms of punishment!

Most parents are punishers. We pay more attention to our child's mistakes, failures and misbehaviors than to his successes, achievements and good behavior! If the kid is behaving, we virtually ignore him. But the minute he misbehaves, we're quick to jump on his case!

FORTIFIED BRATMEAL: The Soggy Cereal Theory

SPOTTY WANTS
FRESH CEREAL

BUT... ALL HE GETS IS
SOGGY CEREAL!

IT ISN'T WHAT SPOTTY
WANTS, OR LIKES, BUT...

EVEN SOGGY CEREAL IS
BETTER THAN NO CEREAL!!

OR, IN OTHER WORDS...

Spotty wants attention. He doesn't care if it's good attention or bad attention because even bad attention is better than no attention! The Spottys of the world learn that being **good** doesn't get very much attention (fresh cereal) from their parents. But being **naughty** gets immediate attention (soggy cereal).

Kids who get a steady diet of soggy cereal keep running back for more!

Now let's look at some **destructive** forms of punishment and see what kinds of nasty problems can arise when parents use punishment as their main means of brat control!

the SPANKING!!

Of all the various forms of punishment, one stands alone—the spanking! We don't know who invented the spanking, or worse yet, who got the very first spanking. But the origin of the spanking goes back a long way. Though possibly accidental in its discovery, the spanking is believed to have soon became a fad. Then it became a sacred ritual that was "handed" down from one generation to the next for centuries. The spanking can still be observed today in remote households where primitive parents believe it is their sacred duty to perform this ancient ritual regularly.

Spanking became so popular that parents quickly exhibited a true poetic flair for announcing its impending execution!* The following are some worthy examples.

Early B.C. era:
"Um ona ank ew!"

Roman Era:
"Et tu, Brute!"

The Dark Ages:
"Shuddup and c'mere!"

Renaissance:
"Bendest thou over, and takest thy medicine!"
"Thou hast begged for it, so thou shall surely now receiveth it!"

The New Dark Ages:
"I'm gonna tan yore hide!"
"When I get done with you, you won't be able to sit down for a month!"
"Shuddup and c'mere!" (Some things never change!)
"I'm gonna bust your britches!" variation: "I'm gonna bust your buns!"
"I'm going to blister your bottom!"
"I'm going to paint your bottom red!"
"I'm gonna whip the living daylights outta you!"
"I'm gonna beat the $%&! out of you!"
"I'm gonna beat the tar outta you!"
"This will teach you a lesson!"
"I don't know why you want me to spank you!"
"This is going to hurt me more than it hurts you!"**

---

*See also *The Scream*, page 48.
**This latter example is attributed to some form of conscience.

TOOLS OF THE TRADE

It is believed most items shown below were employed because of their practicality, regional availability or immediate proximity to angered parents. Because the chief target was the brat's buttocks, practicality and ease of operation have always been prime considerations in selection of a proper tool. Obviously the **hand** is probably the precursor to all the other tools. But because of its own ability to feel pain it hasn't always been a desirable first choice.

B.C. BRAT CONTROL

dinosaur bones

tree branches

clubs or sticks

the handy hand

As man's skills increased throughout history, so did his resourcefulness!
Temperament has truly kept pace with technology, and vice versa!

A.D. (sampling)

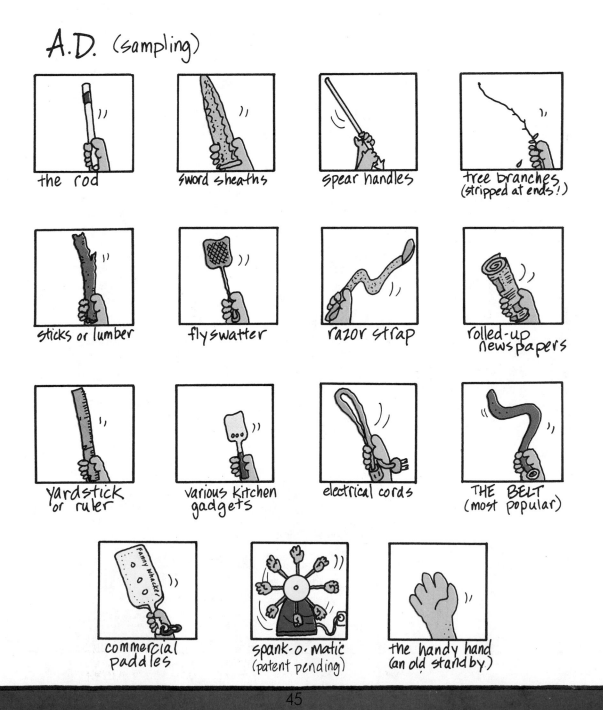

the rod

sword sheaths

spear handles

tree branches (stripped at ends!)

sticks or lumber

fly swatter

razor strap

rolled-up newspapers

yardstick or ruler

various kitchen gadgets

electrical cords

THE BELT (most popular)

commercial paddles

spank-o-matic (patent pending)

the handy hand (an old standby)

It was not until the dawn of the modern era and the invention of child-psy-chologist tricks that the spanking was finally successfully challenged as a valid means of brat control. We know early man, without the aid of books or psychologists, was left to his own devices—and, so, too, were his kids!

So with the sacred spanking ritual on its way to extinction, and knowing violence begets violence, modern man now relies on his keen mind and a wealth of psychological techniques and technology to devise consequences that more fairly, humanely and appropriately fit the crime. We've come a long way, baby! (**Honk,** or more appropriately, **grunt,** if you **don't agree!**)

the scream !!!!!!!....

Any discussion of the spanking must also include the Scream.

Unlike the spanking, the scream never attained any sacredness on its own. (Some believe it becomes sacred when used in conjunction with the Spanking Ritual. This belief is still held and practiced to this day.)

The scream is believed to be the earliest spontaneous reaction ever conveyed by an angered parent. It surely preceded the very first spanking!*

This theory is borne out by the "Shin Test." Two brats, of equal size and ferocity, were asked to kick their parents in the shins **really hard.** In both cases, the **first** reaction was an audible sound, scientifically classifiable as a pure scream.

*Opponents of this theory argue that surprise was the first spontaneous reaction ever conveyed by an angered parent. However, this view is held only by the very naive, the childless or very new parents. No brat's parent is ever surprised by his behavior—they **expect** it! Therefore the Surprise Theory is generally scoffed at in the parentific community at large.

Convenient and reliable, the scream soon surpassed the spanking in popularity and usage. It was especially popular among slow-moving, very lazy parents. It was much easier to scream than to spank!

Though spontaneous at first, the scream soon flourished, and a wide range of vowels and consonants were discovered. These could be used to mean different things! However, a scream was always delivered in a very **loud** manner, accompanied by very ugly facial expressions for necessary emphasis! Instilling fear was the intended result because fear is a great motivator!

As man's language skills increased, so did his perfection of the scream. **Choice words** were added!

This vicious verbosity became known as **screaming, hollering, yelling** and **swearing.** There has been no limit to the depths of man's abusive gleanings or his attendant desire to make ample use of them—with or without provocation!

As man outwardly appeared to become more civilized, screaming and its variations saw a decline in certain elite circles. It soon became common knowledge that only commoners screamed at their brats.

Aristocratic voices were lowered, and words were artfully constructed in such a way as to achieve equally "desirable" results.

It wasn't until the invention of child psychologists that man learned verbal abuse is the first resort of the parentally incompetent and swearing is the only resort of the vocabulary incompetent! Despite man's acquired ability to verbally abuse smaller individuals, it is hoped we shall have this verbal abuse $%&* wiped out!

Meanwhile, the parentally competent are using more-intelligent, positive methods to control behavior!

THE "BEHIND" CONTROL EXPERIMENT

Experiment:
Live brats were exposed to **punishments** (negative consequences) as the only means to attempt to control behavior. No **rewards** or **positive consequences** were used. **Ignoring** was forbidden.

Purpose:
To see what happened!

Subjects:
Five average sets of parents eagerly volunteered for the experiment. Each was assigned a method of punishment to use on their brats. The brats were not told this was an experiment so they weren't prejudiced in any way. The brats ranged in ages from 4 to 17. (Parents wished to remain anonymouse—last names have been omitted.)

Duration·
Experiment ran from December 25 to April 1 of this year.

FAMILY #1	2 brats: Whitey and Spottie

**Method of Punishment:
Screaming & Spankings**

Both kids responded right away by exhibiting fear! **Fear** became the motivator for good behavior. Both brats have physically and emotionally withdrawn from their parents, and it is now unlikely they will ever be close to them. The kids were last observed imitating their parents' behavior in the form of inflicting physical and verbal abuse on each other, their peers and various neighborhood pets.

**Method of Punishment:
Random Discipline**

Both kids quickly felt resentment toward their parents. They felt it wasn't fair not to be advised of the consequences in advance. They were horrified at some of the consequences. Said Tricky, "If I'd known they were going to ground me, I'd never have ate up all the cheese!" Both now feel hatred for their parents, and neither kid feels responsible for his own behavior or consequences. They blame their parents! Both kids are currently expressing anger through a variety of passive-aggressive behaviors—opposition, resistance, stubbornness, defiance, rebellion. Dicky swears some day he's going to tie his parents up and feed them to a cat.

FAMILY #3 | 1 brat: Missy*

Method of Punishment:
Negative Attention
& Verbal Abuse

Missy reacted to this punishment at first by avoiding situations that would lead to more of this type of punishment. She accomplished this by manipulating and lying to her parents. She accidentally broke the cheese dish one day but was so afraid of being punished she lied and denied everything. The constant criticism eventually undermined her self-confidence and made her withdraw from her parents. In desperation she ran away from home. Missy was last seen somewhere in Wisconsin.

(*Missy isn't shown in the photo because she ran away during the experiment.)

FAMILY #4	1 brat: Bully

Method of Punishment:
All types known to man

Nothing fazed Bully! It was amazing. It drove his parents crazy. Punishment couldn't control Bully's behavior because he cared more about the pleasure from the behavior than he did about the consequence for it. (See the Pleasure Seeker, page 122.) Brats like this appear to act before thinking and don't profit from the threat of punishment or past punishment experiences! (It is estimated 3 or 4 kids out of 10 have this personality type.) Bully was transferred to another experiment where Rewards and Ignoring were used for discipline because this is the only method proven to be effective with this personality type. We hear he is now controllable. His parents have recovered and are doing fine.

FAMILY #5 | 4 brats: Mozzy, Swissy, Brie and Ched

Method of Punishment:
Verbal Abuse
(name-calling, screaming,
guilt-induction, belittling)

The variety of responses in the four children included anger, rebellion, withdrawal, bottled emotions, nervousness, guilt, fearfulness and lack of confidence. Negative self-images developed, as did other signs of emotional/personality problems. (The irony is this method was ineffective in controlling the brats' behavior!) Ched's personality type responded the worst to this method. He disclosed he fantasizes often about torturing his parents in various ways. Mozzy is now on a first-name basis with the local police. Brie and Swissy built a better mousetrap for their school science-fair project and have warmly invited their parents to Open House to try it out.

Afterword:
On April 1 the experiment ended. All the parents and kids (except still-missing Missy) were gathered together in one room where the parents then squeaked in unison "April fools!" The kids were not amused.

Now . . . Let's look at some **constructive** forms of punishment! Ironically, "constructive punishment" is not a contradiction in terms—at least not in the following forms! In fact, you'll find these to be quite sporting and fair!

COST PENALTY
Penalizing bad behavior

In other words, the bad behavior "costs" the kid an everyday activity—or even your loving attention! Taking away some activity the brat enjoys, such as watching TV, playing with the computer or listening to the stereo, can be a powerful deterrent! Ahh! The right hand giveth, and the left hand taketh away—but both are the upper hands. (Yours!)

NO PASS, NO PLAY!
Not receiving the reward

With this punishment, the brat doesn't receive something **extra** (a reward). Suppose in exchange for a good behavior you were to offer your brat a reward, a special thing, a privilege or an activity. Then suppose he were to misbehave. Well, the punishment of not receiving the reward (the special thing or privilege) would be its own best punishment! Presto! **Almost any reward can be withdrawn or denied as a means of punishment!**

TIME OUT !!!!

Refereeing the situation

Here's a wonderfully sporting punishment—and an effective one at that! Des-
ignate a **dull place** (such as a corner,
hallway, your accountant's office), and
make the kid stay there for 10 minutes as
time out from a privilege or activity for
bad behavior! (Examples: Turn off TV
cartoons for 10 minutes for your little
ones. Turn off 10 minutes of a dirty movie,
or cartoons, for your teenager!)

Note: When you're a kid, 10 minutes in a dull spot is a loooonnng time!
(You try it!) Besides, studies show 10 minutes is more effective than 1 hour. It
would be better to take away 10 minutes of Saturday cartoons 15 times than
to take away 2-1/2 hours worth once! Don't worry; if the little spoil sport
hasn't scored with the first 10 minutes of inaction, you can always demand
an instant replay!

GO AHEAD... <u>MAKE</u> <u>T</u>HEIR <u>D</u>AY!!!!

Warnings

Should you warn them of their impending doom, or should you just blow them away with it before they know what hits them? Warnings **can** make things run more smoothly and prevent hassles. However, if a clear rule has been brazenly broken, then **take no prisoners!** Otherwise, play it by ear. If you decide to "count 1-2-3," be sure you don't only get to 3 (if behavior persists past 2), but **follow through** once you do. If you don't, your warnings become empty threats and do nothing to stop the behavior. Wouldn't that just make **your** day! While constructive punishment still has its place, modern emphasis is now on a more **positive** approach.

67

68

As the twig is bent, the tree inclines.

Virgil

The best way to keep children home is to make the home atmosphere pleasant, and let the air out of the tires.

Dorothy Parker

Rewards

Positive consequences (rewards) can be described as paying positive attention to the child when he is being good, giving the child something he wants or doing something the child likes or finds enjoyable. In doing this, we pay more attention to the good behavior and less to the bad. This provides the child with an incentive for good behavior. After all, when the consequences for being good outweigh the consequences for being bad, even the most stubborn brat is bound to wise up sooner or later!

71

The Just Desserts

TYPES OF REWARDS

ACTIVITY REWARDS:

Any activity the kid would like. Staying up late, sleep overs with friends, playing games, extra TV time, extended curfews, use of the family car, food fights, wild parties.

SILLY REWARDS:

Any activity or item that parents might think of as silly or a chore. Washing the car, mowing the lawn, helping bake a cake, taking a bubble bath, preparing your IRS return, visiting your mother-in-law.

MATERIAL REWARDS:

Any item the kid might like. Money, toys, candy, snacks, a record album, a sports car, a mink, stock portfolios.

'ANYWAY' REWARDS:

Any item you would get anyway but one you can use as an incentive. New shoes, clothes, a new bedspread, food, shelter, oxygen. (This is sorta sneaky, but don't ya just love it!?)

TOKEN REWARDS:

Something that represents something more important or that can be traded in for a desired object or activity. Stars, stickers, happy-face stickers, checkmarks on a chart. (Warning: Teens do not like happy-face stickers, although stars might be okay if exchangeable for a sports car.)

SOCIAL REWARDS:

(A biggie). This is **free** and always on hand. Praise, hugs, kisses, a smile, laughter, compliments, raves of approval! This is so important; use it constantly and in conjunction with all other rewards! (Tell your 2-year-old how nice she looks in her new mink coat. Tell your 16-year-old how lovely she looks in pink, even if it is her new hair color.)

INTRINSIC REWARDS:

Self-reward, doing it because it feels good, patting yourself on the back. The ultimate goal of all the other rewards is to get the kid to a point where he rewards himself with the best rewards of all—Pride!...Enjoyment!...Smugness!...Conceit!

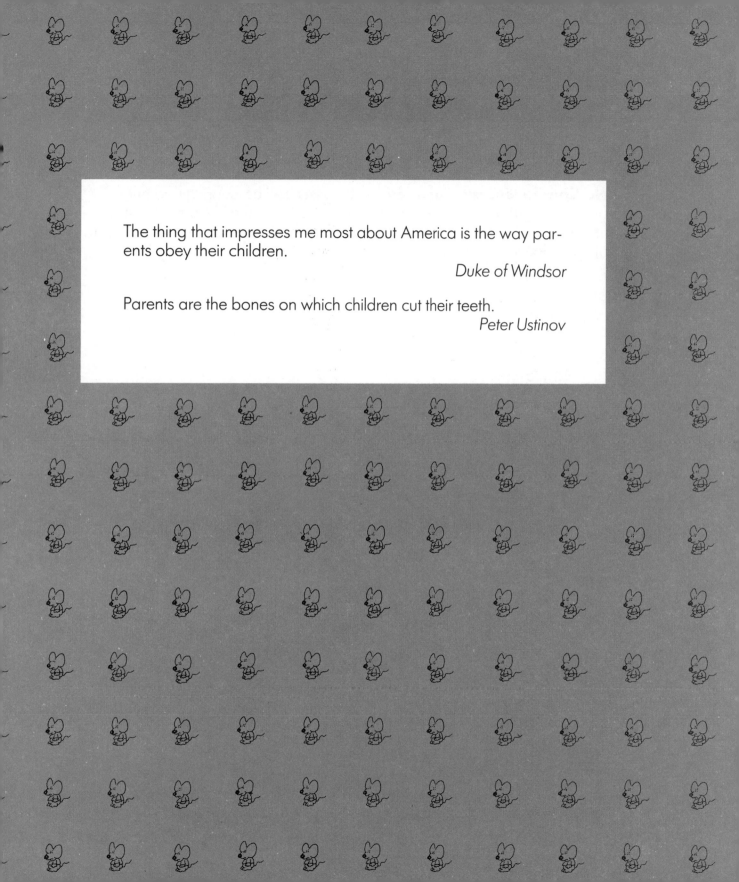

The thing that impresses me most about America is the way parents obey their children.

Duke of Windsor

Parents are the bones on which children cut their teeth.

Peter Ustinov

Ignoring

No Consequences or **Ignoring** can be described as ignoring bad behavior or removing the consequence (parent screaming at the kid, parent getting upset). Ignoring undesirable behavior is a painless, quick, powerful method of discipline in many situations.

No clown will perform without an audience!

STARVE A BRAT,
FEED AN ANGEL

Ignore the tantrum or bad behavior. Reward only good behavior. Reacting to the tantrum only feeds it and makes it grow bigger! (No "soggy cereal," remember!)

Some behaviors in children exist because of the reaction given to them by their parents!

LIFECYCLE OF A TANTRUM

WHAT TO IGNORE

Whatever upsets you or is manipulative. Ignore things the brat does just to make you angry or get your attention. Ignore manipulative behaviors such as:

- whining
- complaining
- pleading
- acting younger than their age
- arguing
- temper tantrums
- faces/dirty looks

WHAT NOT TO IGNORE

Anything task-oriented. Don't ignore a duty, anything that disrupts activities of others or something that may lead to injury or property damage. Don't ignore behaviors such as:

- not doing homework
- hitting anyone
- not cleaning room
- espionage
- stealing plutonium
- TV hogging
- drug dealing
- cat torture

HOW TO DO IT?—CONSISTENTLY!

Plan A:

Withdraw **all** attention, physical or emotional! Pretend the kid is no longer there. Don't look at "it," don't talk to "it." Ignore "it" completely until the behavior stops. Continue about your business, pretending "it" isn't there. Keep chatting with your friend, turn up the TV or stereo, busy yourself with a task, leave the room, leave the house or leave the country! (If the audience leaves, the performance usually ends.)

Plan B:

Withdraw all **emotional** attention, but deal with the behavior. Keep your cool! Resist all impulses to scream, lecture or strangle the little monster. Calmly get on with the business of "rewarding" his naughtiness with "negative consequences"—punishment! (Use Cost Punishment, Time Out!)

Please note—Behavior may worsen or intensify at first, but it does get better if you are **consistent** and **persistent!**

BRAT MODIFICATION CHART

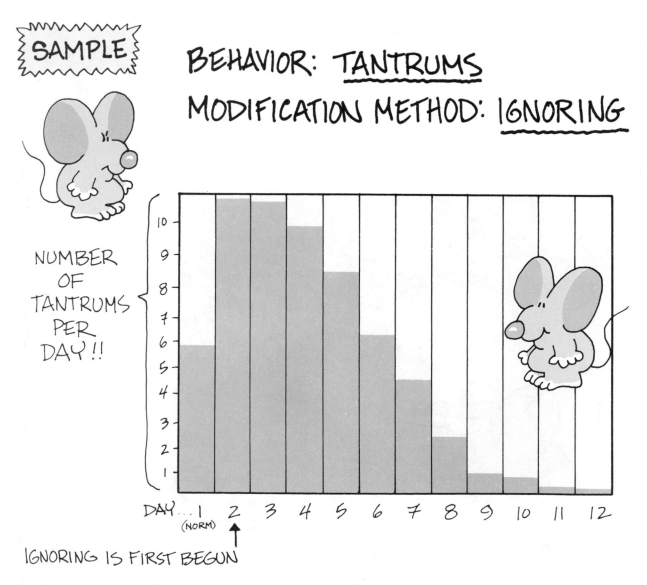

SAMPLE

BEHAVIOR: TANTRUMS

MODIFICATION METHOD: IGNORING

NUMBER OF TANTRUMS PER DAY!!

DAY...1 (NORM) 2 3 4 5 6 7 8 9 10 11 12

IGNORING IS FIRST BEGUN

84

Time Out! ... for a MODERN "VERY TALE"! ...
OUR TALE CONCERNS AN ANGELIC LITTLE GIRL WHO WAS TURNED INTO A HORRIBLE MONSTER BY THE WEAK WILL OF HER PARENTS! THE PARENTS THEN HAD TO CALL UPON THEIR STRONG WILL AND THE MAGICAL POWERS OF A MAGIC ROOM TO HELP CHANGE THEIR DAUGHTER BACK AGAIN!! IT'S CALLED...

ANGEL AND THE MAGIC ROOM

Once upon a time in a suburb, there was born unto this nice couple a beautiful little girl, whom they named Angel, because she looked so sweet and adorable in every way.

Because she was so sweet and adorable, her parents could deny her nothing. They felt they had truly been blessed to have a child of such sweetness and good temperament! And besides, the newness hadn't worn off yet!

Much time passed, and Angel's parents soon noticed that while Angel was still sweet and adorable in every way, her temperament was not! She began to make the most unreasonable wishes and demands of her parents! If they tried to deny even her slightest wish, Angel would whine, scream, throw herself on the floor and thrash wildly about! Although the parents felt like doing the same thing themselves, they wondered what they should really do. And then it happened.

On this particular day, Angel wished to have an ice-cream cone flown in fresh from the North Pole. The parents had grown weary of Angel's wishes. Although they loved her dearly, they decided not to grant this particular wish.

As expected, Angel went into her usual raging tantrum— but this time her parents did nothing! Angel thought maybe her parents hadn't heard her, so she repeated her performance twice as loudly and for twice as long! Her parents still ignored her.

Angel became very, very angry and was about to go into Act III of her performance when her parents took her by her adorable little arms and dragged her down the hallway to a very dull room. They left Angel confused and lying there all alone!

Well, this made Angel 10 times angrier than she'd ever been in her whole life! "You can't make me stay in here!" she screamed as she pulled on the door to get out. But Angel's clever parents were holding the door shut! They kindly told her she could not come out until she decided to stop behaving so badly. Who did they think they were, talking to her that way?! She'd show them.

So Angel screamed louder and pulled and kicked at the door, but still her parents held tightly. This went on for a looonnnng time. Finally, there was silence from within. Angel was ex-hausted. Her head hurt, her feet and hands hurt from kicking and pounding on the door, and her throat was hoarse from screaming. Then Angel heard her parents tell her if she was all finished, she could come out of the dull room. Angel decided this wasn't working anymore anyway, so she agreed.

The door opened, and Angel was greeted by loving hugs and kisses from her parents, who explained to her how sad it made them to put her in the dull room. They hoped she would not make them have to do that to her ever again!

You might think this is the end of the tale! Not really. Angel made other silly wishes and consistently got the same response from her parents. But she did spend less and less time in the dull room! By the end of a fortnight, the sweet, adorable-in-every-way Angel once again had a temperament befitting her name.

To Angel, the dull room **is** a dull room. To her parents, it's the **magic room!** They would probably all be living happily ever after right now except they were audited by the IRS and were caught trying to (illegally) deduct the magic room as an in-house office on their income taxes. The penalties were positively **the end!**

Until you have put yourself into the child's shoes and adjusted your approach to his understanding, you are not communicating at all. You are only talking to yourself.

Unknown

Reasoning with a child is fine—if you can reach the child's reason without destroying your own.

John Mason Brown

Perception
Developing 50-50 Vision

Perceiving can be deceiving! The way you view a situation can make all the difference in the world in understanding and dealing with kids, especially brats! A kid's perception is quite different from yours! Consider this trick question:

Is this kid half-dirty or is he half-clean?

Whose answer is correct?

With this difference in perception, a brat's whole platform for an argument can appear to be quite well-founded, especially in his opinion! And he's willing to articulate his opinion, albeit in a most annoying fashion (arguing, tantrums)! If you, the wiser of the two, can't see **his** side of an issue, then how can you expect this little amoeba to be bright enough to see yours and unquestioningly go along with things?

A good rule to follow is to put yourself in **his** shoes. Try to understand that, right or wrong, he has his opinion and his "reason" for his behavior! This is not to invite reasoning or arguing with the kid—nobody could be that stupid! But by "understanding" his side, it will enable you to function more effectively. You'll be able to see the inspiration behind his position and arguments and objections, and you won't take things so personally. So remember, perception is not our exclusive prerogative!

Now, let's see how this situation progressed. This mom **sees** her dirty little darling's side of the issue, but rather than argue or scream, she uses it to her advantage! Once again, she proves who is the smarter of the species!

the "HOUSEGUESTS"

What if . . . we treated our friends the same way we treat our own children? To find out, we took our cameras to the home of Dodd and Molly Parentice, who fervently believe in the equality of all living matter! They shun the concept of preferential treatment and practice what they preach. They believe one should treat one's friends with the same dignity and respect given to one's children. We learned the Parentices were expecting houseguests for the weekend—their dear friends Billy and Susie Kiddly. As we drop in, we see the Kiddlys arriving . . .

WELCOME

SO,... SUSIE... WHAT HAVE YOU BEEN UP TO?!!
WELL... I'VE RECENTLY GONE BACK TO SCHOOL!
WONDERFUL!!... I ALWAYS THOUGHT YOU NEEDED TO DO THAT! SO...HOW'S IT GOING??
OH... SO FAR I'M MAKING 5 "A's", AND 1 "C"!
THAT'S AWFUL!!! YOU BETTER STUDY HARDER AND PULL THAT "C" UP!!!
WATER

97

99

101

Useless Emotions—
Who needs 'em?

If a glass breaks in the kitchen and you're not there to hear it, does it make a sound?

To find out what effect **useless emotions** have in brat control, parents were asked the following questions:

When was the last time your anger **helped** a situation?
When was the last time your worrying **changed** anything?
When was the last time your getting upset **solved** anything?
When was the last time your screaming **improved** a situation?

Do any of the opposite make you or your brat **feel better?**
Do any of the opposite **improve your relationship?**
Do any of the opposite make you a **better parent?**
Do any of the opposite **improve your health** or the brat's?

103

If someone told you leaving your useless emotions out of brat control would actually improve a situation and your relationship and make you a better more-effective parent, would you **do** it (or work at trying to do it from now on)?

Note—**Do not confuse** displeasure or concern with **anger, worry, getting upset** or **screaming!** It's normal to feel degrees of displeasure and concern, but letting them get out of control and consume you or the situation is the no-no!

Attitude—
It's all in your head

Another way of dealing with a situation is to change your attitude! Your **attitude** about a situation can make a **big** difference in the way you **choose to respond** to it.

The *Cadillac* Cats

Test your attitude-fitness level—Take the following test:
You have just bought a new Cadillac, a white one! You left it sitting out in your driveway overnight! The next day, there are muddy cat prints all over your car! Your reaction would be:

106

IF YOUR ANSWER WAS:

A

What a loser! You're more stupid than a cat to let this bother you! You see something super negative in even the most minor situation! Cars do wash, ya know. So relax! Have your blood pressure checked regularly!

B

How dumb can you be? Cats have a low IQ somewhere between **yours** and a 1-year-old baby! They **don't** know better, and you'll have to catch them first! This attitude gives off bad vibes to you and others.

C

Finally, a smart, sensible, realistic person! Keep telling yourself this as you wash your car off! Very normal, healthy attitude! What a **good** person.

D

This is almost sickeningly **nice** and shows a stunningly **positive** attitude at work (and a charitable one at that)! This is great. You are able to see something positive in almost any situation! But do keep things in perspective. For example, don't say, upon your mother-in-law's accidental death, "Oh well, at least she was insured!"

This simple test helps demonstrate how your attitude directly affects your response! A poor or exaggerated attitude on the front end merely sets you up for a lot of hassles of your own creation. Always tell yourself there are **nicer** things that can happen and there are **worse** things than can happen in **any** situation!! If your brat spilled a glass of milk, be grateful it wasn't the whole carton! If you catch him with a dirty magazine, be grateful you didn't catch him with a dirty girl! And so forth . . . You get the picture! So spare the brat's life and your blood pressure. Shape up that attitude!

COME BACK HERE YOU @#%☆ CATS!!!

Hissssssssss

MMeeeooooowwwww

Perhaps host and guest is really the happiest relation for father and son.

Evelyn Waugh

Parents are the last people on Earth who ought to have children.

Samuel Butler

sofa! A kid is nothing more than a tax-deductible piece of property to do with as you please. They have no rights because they're not **legally** people! Oh sure, when they turn 18 the law says they're adults. I suppose they have rights then, but in the meantime they belong to me. They're too stupid to know what's best for them, so I have to tell them. But don't get me wrong—I love kids! In fact, the greatest thing I like about having kids is how handy they are! When I've had a hard day at the office, there's nothing better than coming home and having a kid there to wait on me, to fetch my paper (they do it better than my dog does), bring me a beer, turn on the television . . . I don't have to lift a finger! I know my wife loves having the kids around. She hasn't had to wash a single dish in years! She's training the youngest to vacuum now, too. She's only 3 years old, and already I can tell she's going to be really handy. I've got my oldest kid balancing my checkbook. The best part is, because they aren't really people yet, they have no human rights. They aren't entitled to be disrespectful or voice their opinions! On the other hand, they can't make their own decisions either. But that's what parents are for—to tell them what to do, how to do it and when to do it. Parents are in total control. I challenge you to show me a set of rules, books or laws that tells me otherwise!

COUNTERPOINT

Josh, you Neanderthal dipstick. I'm surprised your oldest kid hasn't balanced your **body!** Children are not some piece of property we can sit on and write off on our taxes. Unlike you, they are real **people.** A person is a person, regardless of size, age, I.Q. or source of origin—be it the birth canal or the Panama Canal! Giving birth to another human being is not a license to own it and do with it as you please. A child, even a baby, comes with a complete set of inalienable rights—this isn't something he magically or legally acquires at age 18. It's his birthright as a human being. Since when is "parenthood" a license to violate the rights of another human being? Parenthood is a privilege, albeit a sometimes demanding one. It's not easy to take on the enormous responsibility of raising another person. It's very tempting to exercise our physical and psychological dominance over someone smaller and weaker than ourselves! Parents must recognize the "peoplehood" of their children, the progressive adulthood of their children and the rights thereof. They must be willing to respect their children as equals and give them the freedom to disagree, to voice their opinions and to make their own decisions and their own mistakes. We're not here to indenture these little creatures. We're here to give them life and all the riches it has to offer. And, no, you won't find that as a written rule or in any books or laws— it should be a truth we hold self-evident.

The first half of our lives is ruined by our parents and the second half by our children.

Clarence Darrow

We've had bad luck with our kids. They've all grown up.

Christopher Morley

The I'VE·TRIED·EVERYTHING!·NOTHING·WORKS CHECKLIST!!

☐ **Are you primarily using punishment?**
Shame on you! Go stand in the corner for 10 minutes, then . . . switch to **rewards** and **ignoring** to control behavior. See pages 70 and 78.

☐ **Are you being inconsistent?**
Say it isn't so! Stick with a new technique long enough for it to work. Switch techniques only when they become ineffective—or switch **brats** only when they become effective!

Are you overlooking improvements?

Good grief, gimme a break—behavior changes **gradually** not overnight! Look for the slight improvement, and you'll soon realize the behavior has improved 25%, 50% and so forth! By the way, when was your last eye exam anyway?

Are you being fooled?

The little punk is **pretending** not to care about the consequence, and you, thinking it's ineffective, abandon it too early! **Call his bluff!** Hang tough. Take two aspirin, and increase your intake of old Clint Eastwood movies.

Is the consequence important?

If the consequence isn't appropriate for the child, it won't motivate him to change his behavior. You didn't **really** think your 2-year-old would care if you cut him out of your will did you? Get real.

Who are you kidding?

You lazy, lying slob! I bet you haven't **really** even been trying, or you tried for 2 minutes and gave up! You've decided it's much easier to **complain** about the little monster than it is to correct him! Wise up, shut up or see a shrink!

THE SUPERBRAT

Faster than a speeding parent,
More powerful than a loco's motive,
Able to leap all furniture
in a single bound,
Look! Up in the house!

It's a Kid . . .
It's a Brat . . .
It's a SUPERBRAT!

Kraptonite is the only way to deal with these superhuman beings, you say? Then fine, give them some krap tonite. If you've been following along, you know what krap (positive/negative) is available! The only difference between mortal brats and Superbrats is the will of the parents! Superbrats have more stamina and are able to withstand some consequences better and longer than mortal brats. As the parents of a Superbrat, you will frequently be called upon to rise to the occasion and meet the Superbrat head on. You must be stronger mentally than he is and prepared to go the distance! Superbrats lose their superbratual powers when confronted with consistent exposures to Kraptonite! Review all the sections of this book. Increase and customize the dosages and exposures accordingly. And may the Parental Force be with you!

the Pleasure Seeker...

Like Bully in the "Behind" Control Experiment, page 58, this is the sort of brat that is pleasure-oriented or strong-willed. He simply wants to do his own thing, caring more about the pleasure he gets from his behavior than from the consequences. The problem here is most parents attempt to use punishments as the only means to control them. This simply doesn't cut it! The threat of punishment doesn't faze this type of brat nor does past punishment experiences! And (are you sitting down?) because 30 to 40% of all kids have this type personality, chances are pretty good that **your** brat, or one of your brats, may be among these percentages! Frightening but true. You can have one normal brat and one pleasure-seeking brat or, heaven forbid, two or more pleasure-seeking brats! Horrors! What's a parent to do? Practice birth control? (Nice try, but a little late, don't you think?)

   Switch to rewards as a means to control behavior! Rewards provide the pleasure-seeker with a pleasurable incentive for good behavior.

WRONG!!!

RIGHT!!

WRONG!!!

RIGHT!!

Personality-Wise

Let's say you have two kids, a son and a daughter. On the opposite page are some trick questions—answer Yes or No!

If my son became a criminal, I'd feel it was all my fault.

If my daughter became President, I'd feel it was all my fault.

If my son likes the color blue, I'd feel it was all my fault.

If my daughter hates spaghetti, I'd feel it was all my fault.

If my son is shy, I'd feel it was all my fault.

If my daughter is very outgoing, I'd feel it was all my fault.

If my son is musically talented, I'd feel it was all my fault.

If my daughter is very pretty, I'd feel it was all my fault.

If my son became a Republican, I'd feel it was all my fault.

If my daughter became a Democrat, I'd feel it was all my fault.

Heredity explains some things and is a big factor, right? But what if your kid got some errant gene that turns up in your family only every fifth generation? Heredity would be at work, but you'd be mystified just the same! Besides, how can you positively isolate what is **heredity** and what is **environment?**

Reproduction is not a cloning process! Expecting your child or children to be small duplicates of either parent is laughable! Get outta here! Outward appearances may be quite startling. There may be some similar personality traits, but you can bet the little darling has a lot of unique personality traits as well—ones you'll find out about soon as he or she is old enough to "enlighten" you!

Having kids is like random color mixings. One parent with a Red personality plus one parent with a Yellow personality doesn't produce simply one child with red personality traits or one child with yellow personality traits. It produces a whole spectrum of personality traits between red and yellow, over which you have no say and no control.

The **environment** (parents, siblings, home, school, peers, world at large) plays an important yet elusive role, too. Parents are only one part of the environment. You can't possibly expect to be 100% responsible for the outcome of your child! **At best, parents can only hope to affect or modify slightly certain personality traits or behaviors in a child but never totally eliminate or dominate them!** Yet some parents work overtime trying to suppress or dominate the kid's personality and behaviors. They often screw up the kid and the family in this futile endeavor! Even sincere efforts by the parents result in a feeling of guilt and failure. They wonder where **they** went wrong with their child and assume all guilt and blame! They don't stop to consider that maybe even Mother Theresa couldn't have done a better job. Kids can screw up families just as easily as parents can screw up kids! (Imagine if the Beaver had the personality type of Rambo—what would Ward and June have done then? And more importantly, would there have still been a TV series?)

130

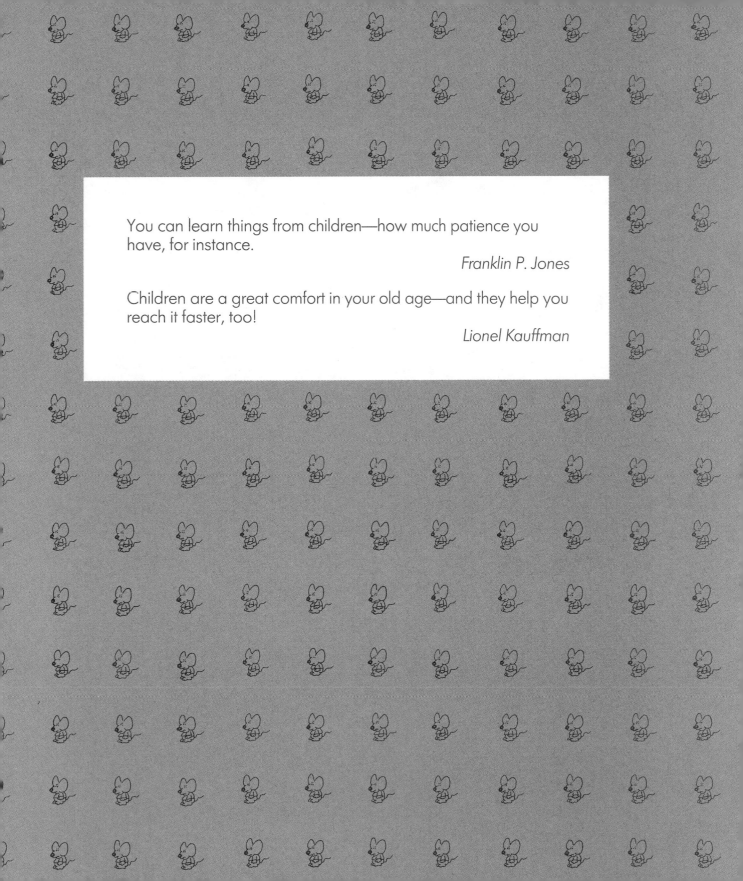

You can learn things from children—how much patience you have, for instance.

Franklin P. Jones

Children are a great comfort in your old age—and they help you reach it faster, too!

Lionel Kauffman

Mom and POP QUIZ !!!!

Have you been paying attention? Did you learn anything? Okay, prove it!

    Below are some multiple-choice questions. Choose the letter that best represents the correct answer. (Good luck)

1. Complete this sentence: "Each child is

a) a future brat!"
b) not a person yet."
c) unique!"

2. This is an example of:

a) a little squealing piggy.
b) a serious warning.
c) a meaningless threat.

3. This is an example of:

a) how to ground a brat.
b) an overstatement.
c) piglet abuse.

4. This is an example of:

a) an attempt at starvation.
b) a hypocritical cat.
c) No = Yes. Saying one thing but doing another.

5. This is an example of:
   a) the "Goldilocks Syndrome."
   b) a beary fitting punishment.
   c) random discipline.

Fill in the Blanks

6. _____ is the foundation of effective child management!
   a) Negotiation   b) Consistency   c) Bribery

7. If we are _____ parents, we increase the chances the techniques we use will work!
   a) generous   b) attractive   c) consistent

8. Our _____ teaches our kids to become confused, not listen and to manipulate us!
   a) arguing   b) inconsistency   c) consistency

9. Consistency and brat eradication come from both parents being _____ .
   a) wishy-washy   b) tough as nails   c) a unit

10. _____ are the most important things in changing behavior!
   a) Ice-cream cones   b) Parents   c) Consequences

11. Three major consequences are: _____ , _____ and _____.
   a) Ignoring, punishments, rewards
   b) Hugs, threats, spankings
   c) Chores, praises, hollering

12. Rules or expectations for behavior should be very _____ .

   a) convenient   b) strict   c) specific

13. This is an example of:
   a) a good threat to enforce curfew.
   b) stupid doggy pastimes.
   c) stating the consequence before the rule is broken.

THE FOLLOWING ARE TRUE OR FALSE STATEMENTS.

Circle T for True and F for False.

T/F 14. Punishments can be described as negative consequences.

T/F 15. There are only destructive forms of punishment.

T/F 16. Most parents pay more attention to bad behavior than to good behavior.

T/F 17. Kids enjoy negative attention.

T/F 18. Spanking is your sacred duty as a parent.

T/F 19. Screaming is very effective at inducing fear and compliance.

T/F 20. Verbal abuse is not as harmful as spanking.

T/F 21. Rewards can be described as positive consequences.

T/F 22. Rewards are a form of bribery.

T/F 23. You will always have to use lots of rewards throughout life.

T/F 24. Intrinsic rewards are the ultimate goal of all rewards.

T/F 25. Cost punishment is the situation in which naughtiness "costs" the kid money.

T/F 26. Rewards should never be withdrawn or denied as a form of punishment.

T/F 27. Time out should last 1 hour or longer.

T/F 28. Ignoring can be described as removing the consequence.

T/F 29. Ignore all bad behavior.

T/F 30. Some behaviors in children exist because of the reaction given to them by their parents.

T/F 31. Ignoring produces positive results immediately.

T/F 32. Some brats don't respond to punishment.

T/F 33. A parent's perception is the only way to view a situation.

T/F 34. Anger, worrying, screaming and getting upset are all necessary emotions for effective parenting.

T/F 35. A negative mental attitude sets you up for a lot of hassles.

Answers are on the following page.

...answers to QUIZ !!!

1. c) Unique
2. c) A meaningless threat
3. b) An overstatement
4. c) No = yes
5. c) Random discipline
6. b) Consistency
7. c) Consistent
8. b) Inconsistency
9. c) A unit
10. c) Consequences
11. a) Ignoring, punishments, rewards
12. c) Specific
13. c) Stating the consequence before the rule is broken.
14. T
15. F (There are also constructive ones!)
16. T (But you know better now, don't you!)
17. F (They prefer good, but bad is better than nothing!)
18. F (If you're a Neanderthal, this is true for you.)
19. T (But why strain those delicate vocal cords?)
20. F (It's the equivalent of a mental spanking!)
21. T

22. F (You weren't paying attention, or you'd have known this one!)
23. F
24. T (I hope you like conceited kids!)
25. F (You didn't fall for this one did you? See #26 below!)
26. F (This is an effective form of "cost punishment!")
27. F (10 minutes. Varies with each personality type.)
28. T
29. F (Some bad behavior is harmful. Some is neglectful of duties!)
30. T
31. F (You wish it did! Behavior intensifies at first but does get better.)
32. T (3 or 4 in 10. Ignoring and rewards must be used instead!)
33. F (A situation can be viewed differently—we didn't say whose was right!)
34. F
35. T

YOUR SCORE

0-10 This is sad! We're hurt! What's the matter, was it the artwork? Do you have the attention span and memory of a goldfish or what? Reread this whole book, but this time with your eyes **open!**

11-15 Okay, you did better than the 0-10 jokers, but less than 50% is nothing to brag about! However, we acknowledge your improvement and admit you are a little better off with this much information than you were before! Please review appropriate sections. Trying to take on brats with only half a load is asking for trouble!

16-24 This is probably about low "average." Whoopie. I know you were probably distracted somewhat by all the great artwork and delightful wit, right? Flattery will get you nowhere! Review the sections you screwed up on, and you'll be glad you did!

25-35 Presuming you didn't cheat, this shows you were indeed paying close attention (or you are lucky and a good guesser!). You are now ready to take on brats of all shapes and sizes consistently and confidently. We pity the poor brats that mess with you! Go get 'em!

Do not mistake a child for his symptoms.

Erik Erikson

To **become** a parent is not hard. To be a parent **is!**

God

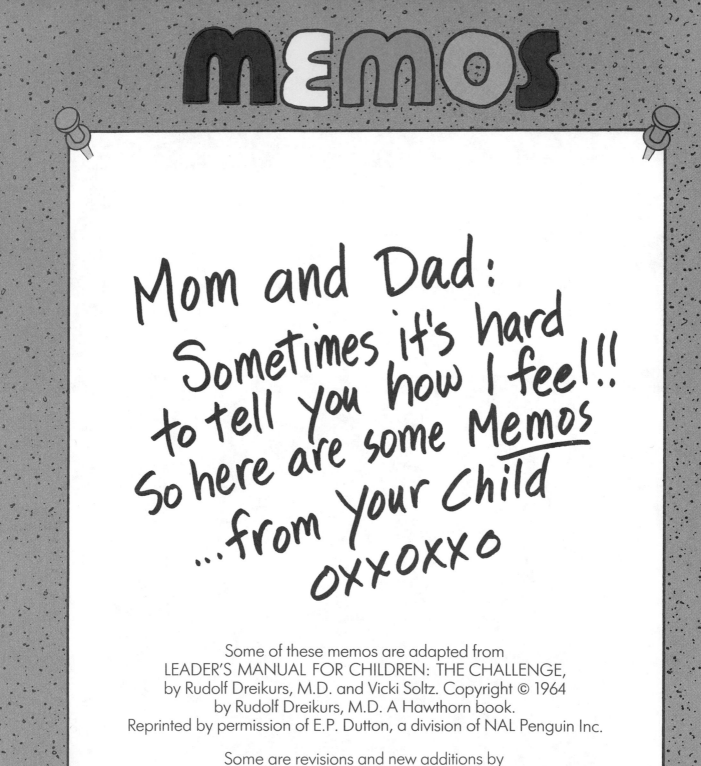

MEMOS

Mom and Dad:
Sometimes it's hard to tell you how I feel!! So here are some Memos ...from your Child OXXOXXO

Some of these memos are adapted from
LEADER'S MANUAL FOR CHILDREN: THE CHALLENGE,
by Rudolf Dreikurs, M.D. and Vicki Soltz. Copyright © 1964
by Rudolf Dreikurs, M.D. A Hawthorn book.
Reprinted by permission of E.P. Dutton, a division of NAL Penguin Inc.

Some are revisions and new additions by
Don H. Fontenelle, Ph.D.

MEMOS

...from your child

DON'T NAG.

If you do, I shall have to protect myself by appearing deaf.

Don't spoil me. I know quite well I ought not to have all I ask for. I'm only testing you.

Don't be afraid to be firm with me. I prefer it. It makes me feel more secure.

Don't let me form bad habits. I have to rely on you to detect them in the early stages.

Don't correct me in front of other people if you can help it. I'll take more notice if you talk quietly with me in private.

Don't make me feel my mistakes are sins. I have to learn to make mistakes without feeling I'm no good.

Don't protect me from consequences. I need to learn from experience.

Don't put me off when I ask honest questions. If you do, you will find I stop asking and seek my information elsewhere.

MEMOS

...from your child

**DON'T ANSWER SILLY OR MEANINGLESS QUESTIONS.
I just want to keep you busy with me!**

Don't use force with me. It teaches me to be aggressive and hostile. I learn power is all that counts.

Don't fall for my provocations when I say and do things just to upset you. If you do, I'll try for more victories.

Don't do things for me I can do for myself. It makes me dependent, and I feel like a baby. I may continue to put you in my service.

Don't let my bad habits get me a lot of attention. It only encourages me to continue them.

Don't think it is beneath your dignity to apologize to me. An honest apology makes me feel surprisingly warm toward you.

Don't forget I love experimenting. I couldn't get on without it, so please put up with it.

MEMOS

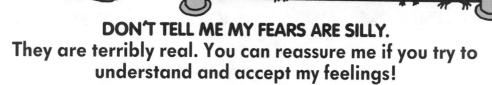

from your child...

> FOR THE LAST TIME: THERE'S NO SUCH THING AS **MONSTERS**!! NOW... GO TO SLEEP YOU SILLY SCAREDY-CAT!!!!

DON'T TELL ME MY FEARS ARE SILLY.
They are terribly real. You can reassure me if you try to understand and accept my feelings!

Don't take too much notice of my small ailments. I may learn to enjoy poor health if it gets me much attention.

Don't forget I can't explain myself as well as I would like to. This is why I'm not always very accurate.

Don't make promises you may not be able to keep. I feel badly let down when promises are broken. This will discourage my trust in you.

Don't tax my honesty too much. I am easily frightened into telling lies.

Don't be inconsistent. That completely confuses me, makes me not listen and teaches me to manipulate you.

Don't try to discuss my behavior in the heat of conflict. For some reason, my hearing is not very good at this time and my cooperation is even worse. It's all right to take the action required, but let's not talk about it until later.

Don't ever suggest you're perfect or infallible. It gives me too much to live up to, as well as too great a shock when I discover you are neither.

MEMOS

...from your child

@#%!!

DON'T PAY MORE ATTENTION TO MY MISTAKES, FAILURES AND MISBEHAVIORS THAN TO MY SUCCESSES, ACCOMPLISHMENTS AND GOOD BEHAVIORS.

**I need lots of understanding, encouragement and positive attention.
I can't pat myself on the back.
I rely heavily on you to do this.**

Don't let my fears arouse your anxiety. If they do, I will become more afraid. Show me courage.

Don't be too upset when I say "I hate you." I don't mean it, but I want you to feel sorry for what you have done to me.

Don't forget how quickly I am growing up. It must be very difficult to keep pace with me, but please try. Don't try to preach to me. You'd be surprised at how well I know what's right and wrong.

Don't demand explanations for my wrong behavior. I really don't know why I did it.

Treat me the way you treat your friends, then I will be your friend, too. I learn more from a model than a critic.

GLOSSARY
of Common
Ailments of Parenting

Major Ailments

Compensationitis: Common condition affecting all parents who think they can make up to their child for things they never got when they were young. They try to treat their child better than their parents treated them. Promotes spoiling. Results in bewildered parents who wonder how their child can be so ungrateful and unappreciative of all the wonderful things given him and done for him, things the parent would have died for as a child!

Ignoratosis: Sometimes-terminal condition whereby a parent (or parents) ignores his child's behavior, be it bad behavior or **good** behavior. Severest form—ignoring your child! Promotes super-brattiness and alienation of affection. Carries with it the possibility of one day seeing your child's photo in the post office on the FBI'S Most-Wanted list.

Disciplinaria: Cruel malady affecting parents who think the only way to change a child's behavior is through strict discipline and punishment. This Neanderthal form of child rearing results in frustration and alienation for children and parents—and the ghastly prospect of retaliation by your teenage son the day he becomes taller than you!

Inconsistentosis: One of the most common, serious ailments of parenthood. The act of one or both parents being inconsistent with their child. Extremely harmful. Produces brats of the most obnoxious variety known to man or animals! Promotes failure in child-rearing, undermines disciplinary tactics, **guarantees** disharmony in the home and breeds many of the following related ailments.

Related Ailments

Hollermania—Disgusting, noisy habit. The tactless ability of raising one's voice too many decibels to berate or command the attention of the child. Often accompanies or precedes Disciplanaria or Criticizosis.

Screamsalotitis—Closely related to Hollermania, but a few decibels higher. Resorted to more frequently. Exhibits total loss of control of a situation. Mostly conducted in a spontaneous frenzy, without premeditated intellectual thought.

Nag-o-mania—Used by itself, or combined with Hollermania or Scream-salotitis, Nag-o-maniacs can drive themselves and their children crazy with constant nagging. Especially effective and destructive when combined with Criticizosis. Believed to be self-perpetuating.

Criticizosis—Finding fault with one's child. Especially harmful if used in excess, without the façade of constructiveness. Prolonged usage results in low self-image for children, which they feel compelled to "live up to."

Worryphobia—Pervasive condition affecting parents **all** their lives. The malady of worrying about one's child. Normal in most cases. Not curable but controllable. Harmful and debilitating to adult and child if condition becomes excessive. A friend to ulcers.

Upsetitis—Condition brought on parents by themselves. They allow themselves to get upset over real or imaginary things their children do or don't do. Harmful to adult and child. Serves little purpose other than to enrich pharmaceutical companies. Sometimes seen in conjunction with Worryphobia. Usually precedes any of the above and can be very destructive when used in conjunction with most of the above.

CONGRATULATIONS!! AND REMEMBER... WHILE THERE IS NO SUCH THING AS A **PERFECT PARENT** THERE **IS** SUCH A THING AS A **BETTER PARENT!!** BUT BECOMING A BETTER PARENT ISN'T AN OVERNIGHT THING!! IT TAKES TIME, CONSISTENCY, PATIENCE AND LOTS OF LOVE!!! SO FROM TIME TO TIME PLEASE REREAD THIS BOOK! IT WILL REFRESH YOUR MEMORY, SHARPEN YOUR SKILLS AND KEEP YOUR SENSE OF HUMOR INTACT!!! **THANKS**... AND **HAPPY PARENTING!!!!!!**

About the Authors

Beverly Guhl is an insightful mother of two children. A humorist with a worldwide reputation, Beverly's wit and characters have appeared on greeting cards, bookmarks, mugs, magnets and other products in the U.S. and Europe. Additionally, she has done record-album covers, coauthored an animated video for children and licensed her posters.

"Why did I write this book? Because I am a child-psychology aficionado (aren't we all?), and I have been using all the techniques in a humorously serious but seriously humorous way while raising my two children! In fact, my kids are such shining examples that strangers would stop me on the street and ask how they could have such angels! Kidnapping being illegal, I would recommend books (and/or shrinks), but most people were too busy (a few were just too lazy)!!! I decided to do something drastic—I created, wrote and illustrated this book!

"Far too busy (or lazy) to obtain a Ph.D. of my own, I got a real child psychologist, Don Fontenelle, Ph.D., to provide me with the sound psychological principles upon which I based most of this book! All I ask is that nobody hold me, Dr. Fontenelle or Fisher Books responsible if they become a better, happier parent after reading and using this book! Okay? Thanks!!"—*Beverly Guhl*

Don H. Fontenelle, Ph.D., is a child/adolescent psychologist who is in private practice in the New Orleans area. Most of his career has been directed toward providing parents with a better understanding of their children and ways to deal with their children's behavior. He has written several books on the subject of child behaviors and parenting. These include *How to Live with your Children,* Almar Press, 1981; *Changing Student Behavior,* Shenkman Publishing, 1982; and *Understanding and Managing Over-Active Children,* Front Row Experience, 1987.

INDEX